THE
COOKIE
LOVERS
COOKIE
COOKBOOK

by
PRUDENCE MADDEN YOUNGER

drawings by SUSAN SWAN

Published by
The Trumpet Club
666 Fifth Avenue
New York, New York 10103

ISBN: 0-440-84056-2

Printed in the United States of America
November 1988

10 9 8 7 6 5 4 3 2

KRI

*To Millicent and Stephen,
who provided the inspiration
for this book
and the opportunity
to write it*

AUTHOR'S NOTE

EVERYBODY LOVES COOKIES. Some people get stuck on one kind, while others have two or three favorites that they hope are in the cookie jar. There are some people, however, who love all kinds of cookies; and if you are one of them, this book is especially for you. The recipes and easy instructions show you how to create 35 different cookie masterpieces for your family and friends—whether you are a good baker already or are just starting out.

Gaydance Madden Younger

CONTENTS

EASY NO-BAKE TREATS

COOKIES FOR SPECIAL OCCASIONS

FUN WITH COOKIES

RULES FOR SUCCESS IN THE KITCHEN

Success in the kitchen depends upon following certain rules.

Rule 1 Be a considerate cook; always ask for permission before you start. If you do, you will avoid conflict, in case someone else is planning to use the kitchen. Show your mom or dad the recipe you would like to make. If the recipe says that you might need some help, ask for it before you start to cook.

Rule 2 Read the recipe all the way through. You don't want any surprises! Make sure that you have everything you will need to make the cookies, or that you have permission to buy ingredients or utensils that you do not have.

Rule 3 Wash your hands! Always have clean hands before you touch ingredients or utensils. This is one step that you cannot repeat too many times. Nobody wants to eat dirty cookies—especially you. If you have long hair, now is a good time to pull it back or put it into a braid so that a stray hair won't get in your way—or into your cookies. You may want to put out the cat or dog, too.

Rule 4 Line up all the things that you will need on the counter. Then, as you finish with each item, put it away or off to one side. This way you'll be sure to put everything in, and you won't add anything twice.

Rule 5 Measure all the ingredients exactly. The recipes tell how much of everything to use. If you follow a recipe exactly, the cookies will come out the way they are supposed to. (A separate section on ingredients and equipment appears at the end of this book.)

Rule 6 Set the oven carefully. The temperature of the oven determines how quickly or slowly the cookies bake. Have an adult show you how to set the oven at the right temperature. And remember to turn off the oven (or the stove burner) as soon as you have finished using it.

Rule 7 Before you pick a hot pan up, know where you are going to put it down. The worst dilemma that a baker can face is taking a hot pan of cookies from the oven and not having a place to put it down. Clear a spot before you open the oven door.

Rule 8 *Always* use potholders when putting pans into the oven or taking pans out of the oven. There is no sense ruining your baking fun with burnt fingers.

Rule 9 When you are through baking, clean up the kitchen. This may seem like the simplest rule, but it is the most important. If you leave a mess, you may not be allowed to cook again. Put things away as you finish using them. Wash up the dishes while your cookies bake. No matter how you do it, leave the kitchen neat, clean, and orderly.

Rule 10 Store your finished cookies carefully. It would be a shame to bake a perfect batch of cookies only to have them go stale before you could enjoy them. Bar cookies should be individually wrapped in plastic wrap or aluminum foil. Crisp cookies should be stored in a container with a tightly fitting lid. Chewy cookies should be put in a tightly covered container also, but put a piece of apple in with the cookies to keep them chewy. Store each different kind of cookie in its own container, so the flavors will stay separate and distinct.

A good trick is to wrap cookies individually and store them in the freezer. If you take a frozen cookie out in the morning and put it in your lunch box, it will be thawed and taste freshly baked by noon.

FAVORITE BAR COOKIES

Bar cookies are easy to make because you just spread the dough into the pan and put it in the oven. Bar cookies are especially good for bake sales because you can cut the cookies to be as big or as small as you want.

DOUBLE FUDGE BROWNIES

These brownies are extra special and extra fudgy because they have chocolate chips in the batter.

YOU WILL NEED

A large saucepan
A wooden spoon
A 13 × 9-inch baking pan, greased
A rubber scraper

4 ounces (4 squares) unsweetened chocolate
1 cup (2 sticks) butter or margarine
2 cups sugar
4 eggs
1 teaspoon vanilla
1¼ cups flour
1 teaspoon baking powder
1 teaspoon salt
1 cup (6-ounce package) semi-sweet chocolate chips

PREHEAT OVEN TO 350 DEGREES (325 DEGREES IF USING A GLASS PAN)

Put the chocolate and the butter or margarine in the saucepan. Place over low heat and stir with the wooden spoon until the chocolate has melted. Remove the saucepan from the heat and turn the burner off. Stir in the sugar, eggs, and vanilla. Stir in the flour, baking powder, and salt. Add the chocolate chips and stir. Put the batter into the greased baking pan. Make sure you scrape the sides of the saucepan with the rubber scraper to get all of the batter. Put the baking pan in the oven and bake for 35 minutes, or until the brownies begin to pull away from the sides of the pan. When the cookies are done, take the pan out of the oven. Allow the brownies to cool in the pan before cutting into bars.

YIELD: 12 really big brownies or 24 smaller ones

BLONDE BROWNIES (BLONDIES)

Rich and chewy like their chocolatey cousins, these brown sugar "blondies" are certain to win applause from everybody who tastes them.

YOU WILL NEED

A large saucepan
A wooden spoon
A 9-inch-square baking pan, greased

½ cup (1 stick) butter or margarine
1 cup brown sugar, packed
2 eggs
1 teaspoon vanilla
1½ cups flour
2 teaspoons baking powder
½ teaspoon salt

PREHEAT OVEN TO 350 DEGREES (325 DEGREES IF USING A GLASS PAN)

Put the butter or margarine in the saucepan. Place over low heat until the butter or margarine melts. Remove the pan from the heat and turn the burner off. Use the wooden spoon to stir in the brown sugar, eggs, and vanilla. Stir in the flour, baking powder, and salt. Mix well. Spread the batter evenly into the greased pan. Bake the cookies for 30 to 35 minutes or until the batter begins to pull away

15

from the sides of the pan. Remove the pan from the oven. Allow the blondies to cool for about 15 minutes before cutting into bars.

YIELD: 9 really big blondies or 18 smaller ones

PEANUT BUTTER BARS

This chewy peanut butter bar has a crunch that comes from real peanuts.

YOU WILL NEED

A large mixing bowl
A wooden spoon
A 9-inch-square baking pan,
   greased

2 eggs
1 cup sugar
½ cup brown sugar, packed
½ cup peanut butter
1 teaspoon vanilla
1½ cups flour
2 teaspoons baking powder
1 cup salted peanuts

PREHEAT OVEN TO 350 DEGREES (325 DEGREES IF USING A GLASS PAN)

Put the eggs, sugar, brown sugar, and peanut butter in the mixing bowl, and blend together using the wooden spoon. Stir in the vanilla, flour, and baking powder. Stir in the peanuts. Spread the batter evenly into the greased baking pan. Put the pan in the oven and bake for 30 minutes or until the batter begins to pull away from the sides of the pan. Remove the pan from the oven. Allow the cookies to cool before cutting into bars.

YIELD: 9 large bars or 18 smaller ones

TROPICAL TOFFEE BARS

Crunchy coconut topping and a rich butter-scotch crust make these chewy bars doubly delicious. They look like they are hard to make; but they are really very easy, and are a favorite among adults as well as kids.

YOU WILL NEED

A mixing bowl
A wooden spoon
A 13 × 9-inch baking pan

For the Crust
½ cup (1 stick) butter or
   margarine, softened
½ cup brown sugar, packed
1 cup flour

For the Topping
2 eggs
1 cup brown sugar, packed
1 teaspoon vanilla
2 tablespoons flour
1 teaspoon baking powder
1 cup shredded coconut
½ cup chopped walnuts

PREHEAT OVEN TO 350 DEGREES (325 DEGREES IF USING A GLASS PAN)

Put the softened butter or margarine and the ½ cup of brown sugar in the mixing bowl, and blend them together using the wooden spoon. Stir in 1 cup of flour. The mixture will be soft and a little crumbly. Use your fingertips to press the mixture evenly into the bottom of the baking pan. Put the baking pan in the oven and bake for 10 minutes.

While the crust is baking, prepare the topping. Put the eggs, 1 cup of brown sugar, the vanilla, the

2 tablespoons of flour, and the baking powder into the mixing bowl. (You don't have to wash out the mixing bowl first.) Mix well. Stir in the coconut and the chopped walnuts.

When the crust has finished baking, take the pan out of the oven, but leave the oven on. Leave the crust in the pan. Carefully spread the coconut mixture over the crust. Return the pan to the oven and bake for 25 minutes more. Remove the pan from the oven. Allow the cookies to cool for 15 minutes before cutting into bars.

YIELD: 36 bars

JAM STICKS

Use your favorite jam as the filling for these chewy bar cookies. Strawberry, raspberry, peach, or apricot—the possibilities are many.

YOU WILL NEED

A large mixing bowl
A wooden spoon
A 13 × 9-inch baking pan, greased
A rubber scraper

¾ cup (1 and ½ sticks) butter or margarine, softened
1 cup brown sugar, packed
2 cups flour
½ teaspoon salt
½ teaspoon baking soda
1¼ cups quick, uncooked rolled oats
1 cup jam

PREHEAT OVEN TO 400 DEGREES (375 DEGREES IF USING A GLASS PAN)

Put the butter or margarine and the brown sugar in the mixing bowl and blend together using the wooden spoon. Stir in the flour, salt, baking soda, and oats. Mix well. The mixture will be crumbly. Put half the mixture into the pan. Pat it down evenly to form the bottom "crust." Spread the jam evenly over the mixture in the pan. Use the rubber scraper to make sure that the jam is in an even layer. Take the remaining dough and sprinkle it over the jam. It should be crumbly. Put the pan in the oven and bake for about 30 minutes. Remove the pan from the oven. Cool for 10 minutes before cutting into bars.

YIELD: 36 bars

S'MORE BARS

You don't need an open fire to make this variation of a favorite camping treat.

YOU WILL NEED

An 8-inch-square baking pan

¼ cup (½ stick) butter or margarine
1 cup graham cracker crumbs
¾ cup sweetened condensed milk
1 cup (6-ounce package) milk-chocolate chips
2 cups miniature marshmallows (or large marshmallows, cut up)

PREHEAT OVEN TO 350 DEGREES (325 DEGREES IF USING A GLASS PAN)

Put the butter or margarine into the baking pan and place it in the oven for 3 minutes or until the butter or margarine is melted. Take the pan out of the oven, and sprinkle the graham cracker crumbs evenly over the melted butter. Pour the sweetened condensed milk evenly over the graham cracker crumbs. Sprinkle the milk-chocolate chips evenly over the milk. Spread the marshmallows in a layer over the milk-chocolate chips. Use your fingers to press down evenly on the marshmallows. Put the pan in the oven and bake for 30 minutes.

Remove the pan from the oven. Let the s'mores cool completely before cutting into squares.

YIELD: 16 squares

DROP COOKIES

Some of the all-time favorite cookies are drop cookies, like chocolate chip and oatmeal raisin. You just drop globs of the cookie dough onto the cookie sheet and bake. Most of these recipes are easy for beginning bakers.

GIANT CHOCOLATE CHIPPERS

These are probably the best chocolate chip cookies you'll ever eat. You can make 12 giant cookies, as it says in the recipe, or 24 smaller cookies. Either size tastes out of this world.

YOU WILL NEED

A large mixing bowl
A wooden spoon
Greased cookie sheets

¼ cup (½ stick) butter or
    margarine, softened
¼ cup shortening
½ cup sugar
¼ cup brown sugar, packed
1 egg
1 teaspoon vanilla
1⅓ cups flour
1 teaspoon baking soda
½ cup chopped walnuts
½ cup semi-sweet chocolate
    chips
⅓ cup shredded coconut

PREHEAT OVEN TO 375 DEGREES

Put the butter or margarine, shortening, sugar, and brown sugar into the mixing bowl. Blend together using the wooden spoon. Stir in the egg and vanilla. Stir in the flour and baking soda. Mix well. Stir in the nuts, chocolate chips, and coconut. Mix well. Drop the dough in 12 equal piles onto a greased cookie sheet. Use your hand to flatten each pile slightly. Place the cookie sheet on the lowest rack in the oven. Bake for 15 minutes. When the cookies are done, take the cookie sheet from the oven. Allow the cookies to cool for a few minutes before removing them from the cookie sheet.

YIELD: 12 large cookies

NOTE To make smaller cookies, drop the dough by teaspoonfuls onto the greased cookie sheet. Leave 3 inches between the cookies and bake 12 minutes. This makes 24 small cookies.

OLD-FASHIONED OATMEAL RAISIN COOKIES

Chewy and sweet, these favorites have been around for a long, long time. Try them warm from the oven with an icy cold glass of milk.

YOU WILL NEED

A large mixing bowl
A wooden spoon
Greased cookie sheets

PREHEAT OVEN TO 350 DEGREES

¾ cup shortening
½ cup brown sugar, packed
1 egg
¼ cup milk
½ teaspoon baking soda
½ teaspoon salt
1 teaspoon vanilla
1 cup flour
1 cup raisins
3 cups quick, uncooked rolled oats

Put the shortening, brown sugar, and egg into the bowl, and blend well using the wooden spoon.

Add the milk, baking soda, salt, vanilla, and flour to the bowl, and stir everything well. Stir in the raisins and oats. Drop by teaspoonfuls onto the greased cookie sheets. Leave 2 to 3 inches between each cookie. Put in the oven and bake for 15 minutes or until the cookies begin to turn golden brown around the edges. When the cookies are done, take them out of the oven. Use a pancake turner to lift the cookies from the cookie sheet and onto a rack to cool.

YIELD: 36 cookies

SCOTCH DROPS

Loaded with butterscotch bits, these chewy cookies are bound to make a butterscotch lover out of anyone.

YOU WILL NEED

A large saucepan
A wooden spoon
Greased cookie sheets

¼ cup (½ stick) butter or margarine
1 cup brown sugar, packed
1 egg
1 teaspoon vanilla
1 teaspoon baking powder
½ teaspoon salt
1 cup flour
1 cup (6-ounce package) butterscotch bits

PREHEAT OVEN TO 375 DEGREES

Put the butter or margarine into the saucepan. Place over low heat until the butter or margarine has melted. Remove the saucepan from the heat

24

and turn the burner off. Stir in the brown sugar, egg, vanilla, baking powder, salt, and flour. Mix well. Stir in the butterscotch bits, and mix well. Drop the dough by teaspoonfuls 3 inches apart on a greased cookie sheet. Place in the oven and bake for 10 minutes. When the cookies are done, take the cookie sheet from the oven. Let the cookies cool for a few minutes before removing them from the cookie sheet.

YIELD: 36 scotch drops

JEWELED JUMBLES

Gum drops mixed into the cookie dough make these drop cookies look like they are full of precious jewels.

YOU WILL NEED

Clean scissors
A large mixing bowl
A wooden spoon
Ungreased cookie sheets

2 cups gumdrops
1 teaspoon flour to coat the gumdrops
1/3 cup shortening
1/3 cup margarine, softened
1/2 cup sugar
1/2 cup brown sugar, packed
1 egg
1 teaspoon vanilla
1 3/4 cups flour
1/2 teaspoon baking soda
1/4 teaspoon salt

PREHEAT OVEN TO 350 DEGREES

Use the clean scissors to cut the gumdrops up into small pieces. Put the cut-up gumdrops into a

25

small plastic bag with a teaspoon of flour, and shake to coat the gumdrops. Put the shortening, margarine, sugar, and brown sugar into the mixing bowl, and blend together using the wooden spoon. Stir in the egg and vanilla. Stir in the flour, baking soda, and salt. Stir in the cut-up gumdrops. Drop the dough by teaspoonfuls onto the cookie sheet, leaving 2 inches between each cookie. Put in the oven and bake for 10 minutes. When the cookies are done, take the cookie sheet from the oven. Allow the cookies to cool slightly before removing them from the cookie sheet.

YIELD: 36 cookies

PROSPECTOR COOKIES

Peanut butter chips appear like gold nuggets buried in each of these miniature chocolate mountains.

YOU WILL NEED

A large mixing bowl
A wooden spoon
Greased cookie sheets

½ cup shortening
1 cup sugar
1 egg
1¼ teaspoons baking soda
½ cup unsweetened
   powdered cocoa
1 teaspoon vanilla
2 cups flour
1 cup milk
1 cup (6-ounce package)
   peanut butter chips

PREHEAT OVEN TO 375 DEGREES

26

Put the shortening, sugar, and egg into the bowl, and blend together using the wooden spoon. Stir in the baking soda, cocoa, vanilla, flour, and milk. Stir in the peanut butter chips. Drop the dough by teaspoonfuls onto the greased cookie sheets, leaving 2 inches between each cookie. Put the cookies into the oven and bake for 12 minutes. When the cookies are done, take the cookie sheet from the oven. Let the cookies cool a little before removing them from the cookie sheet.

YIELD: 36 cookies

FORGOTTEN COOKIES

Put these cookies into the oven before you go to bed at night—and try to forget about them until morning! When you open the oven the next day, a pleasant surprise will greet you.

YOU WILL NEED

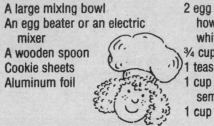

A large mixing bowl
An egg beater or an electric mixer
A wooden spoon
Cookie sheets
Aluminum foil

2 egg whites (see page 89 for how to separate egg whites)
¾ cup sugar
1 teaspoon vanilla
1 cup (6-ounce package) semi-sweet chocolate chips
1 cup chopped pecans

PREHEAT OVEN TO 350 DEGREES

Use the aluminum foil to line the cookie sheet. Put the egg whites into the mixing bowl. Use the

27

electric mixer or egg beater to beat the egg whites until they are foamy and full of bubbles. Continue beating, adding the sugar a little bit at a time as you beat. When all the sugar is added and the egg whites are stiff enough to form stiff peaks, turn off the electric beater and unplug it. Use the wooden spoon to stir the vanilla, the chocolate chips, and the nuts into the egg-white mixture. Drop the mixture by teaspoonfuls onto the foil-covered cookie sheet. Place the cookie sheet in the oven. NOW TURN THE OVEN OFF. Do not open the oven door until morning.

YIELD: 36 cookies

NOTE These cookies cannot be frozen.

MOLDED
COOKIES

With molded cookies you use your hands to form the dough into the size and shape that you want. The dough is stiff so that you can roll it in a sugar coating before baking; that's how snickerdoodles and molasses chews get their crunchy crusts. You can also shape this kind of cookie dough around other things before baking, like the chocolate kisses for inside-out peanut butter cups.

INSIDE-OUT
PEANUT BUTTER CUPS

These peanut-butter-flavored cookies are each topped with a chocolate kiss that does not melt while the cookie bakes. What a surprise to see the little mountains of milk chocolate emerge from the hot oven!

YOU WILL NEED

A large mixing bowl
A wooden spoon
Greased cookie sheets

PREHEAT OVEN TO 375 DEGREES

¼ cup shortening
¼ cup (½ stick) butter or
    margarine, softened
½ cup peanut butter
½ cup sugar
⅓ cup brown sugar, packed
1 egg
½ teaspoon vanilla
1¼ cups flour
½ teaspoon baking powder
¾ teaspoon baking soda
36 chocolate kisses,
    unwrapped

Put the shortening, softened butter or margarine, the peanut butter, the sugar, and the brown sugar into the mixing bowl. Blend them together using the wooden spoon. Stir in the egg and vanilla. Stir in the flour, baking powder, and baking soda. Use your hands to shape the dough into 1-inch balls and place them on the greased cookie sheet. Leave 2 inches between each cookie ball. Press a chocolate kiss onto the top of each ball. The cookie should flatten out slightly. Put the cookies into the oven and bake them for 12 minutes or until the bottoms of the cookies begin to turn golden brown. Use a pancake turner to tip a cookie so you can see underneath. When the cookies are done, take the cookie sheet from the oven. Use the pancake turner to lift the cookies onto a rack to cool.

YIELD: 36 cookies

MOLASSES CHEWS

These chewy molasses cookies are spicy like gingersnaps and have a crinkly sugar top.

YOU WILL NEED

A large mixing bowl
A wooden spoon
Greased cookie sheets
A saucer

¾ cup shortening
1 cup brown sugar, packed
1 egg
¼ cup light or dark molasses
2 cups flour
2 teaspoons baking soda
1 teaspoon ground cloves
1 teaspoon ground cinnamon
1 teaspoon ground ginger
1 tablespoon sugar

Put the shortening, brown sugar, egg, and molasses into the mixing bowl, and blend them together using the wooden spoon. Stir in the flour, baking soda, cloves, cinnamon, and ginger. Mix thoroughly. Cover the bowl of dough with plastic wrap or waxed paper and place it in the refrigerator

31

to chill for about an hour. While the dough is chilling, wash the dishes. Put the tablespoon of sugar into the saucer.

PREHEAT OVEN TO 375 DEGREES

Take the dough out of the refrigerator and use your hands to shape it into 1-inch balls. Dip the top of each ball into the sugar in the saucer, and place the balls 3 inches apart on the baking sheet, sugar side up. Use your fingertips to sprinkle 2 or 3 drops of water onto the sugar on top of each cookie. Put the cookies in the oven and bake for about 10 minutes or until they just begin to turn brown around the edges. Take the cookie sheet from the oven. Use a pancake turner to lift the cookies from the cookie sheet and onto a rack to cool.

YIELD: 40 cookies

SNICKERDOODLES

These buttery cookies have a funny name that might make you laugh. The real smiles will come when you taste their cinnamon flavor.

YOU WILL NEED

A large mixing bowl
A wooden spoon
Ungreased cookie sheets
A saucer

½ cup (1 stick) butter or
    margarine, softened
¾ cup sugar
1 egg
1 teaspoon cream of tartar
½ teaspoon baking soda
1½ cups flour
1 teaspoon ground cinnamon
1 tablespoon sugar

PREHEAT OVEN TO 400 DEGREES

Put the softened butter or margarine and the ¾ cup of sugar into the mixing bowl. Blend them together thoroughly with the wooden spoon. Stir in the egg. Stir in the cream of tartar, baking soda, and flour.

Put the cinnamon and the tablespoon of sugar into the saucer and mix them together.

With your hands, shape the cookie dough into 1-inch balls. Roll each ball in the cinnamon-sugar mixture, and place the balls on the cookie sheet. Leave 2 inches between each ball.

Put the cookies in the oven and bake for 8 to 10 minutes or until the bottoms of the cookies begin to turn golden brown. Use a pancake turner to tip a cookie so you can see underneath. When the cookies are done, take the cookie sheet from the oven.

Use the pancake turner to lift the cookies from the cookie sheet and onto a rack to cool.

YIELD: 30 snickerdoodles

SNOWBALLS

The sugar coating on these little butterballs melts like snow in summer when you put the cookie into your mouth.

YOU WILL NEED

A large mixing bowl
A wooden spoon
A greased cookie sheet
A saucer
A plate

½ cup (1 stick) butter or
  margarine, softened
½ cup powdered sugar
1 teaspoon vanilla
1 cup flour
¼ cup powdered sugar to roll
  the finished cookies in

PREHEAT OVEN TO 400 DEGREES

Put the softened butter or margarine into the mixing bowl. Using the wooden spoon, blend the ½ cup of powdered sugar into the butter or margarine. Stir in the vanilla. Gradually stir in the flour. The dough will get crumbly as the flour is added, so you may need to use your hands to get the flour thoroughly blended in. Use your hands to form the dough into 1-inch balls and place them 1 inch apart on the cookie sheet. Put the cookies into the oven and bake for 10 minutes or until the bottoms of the cookies begin to turn golden brown. Use a pancake turner to tip a cookie so you can see underneath.

While the cookies are baking, put the ¼ cup of powdered sugar into the saucer.

When the cookies are done, take them out of the oven. Use the pancake turner to lift the cookies from the cookie sheet, and put them onto the plate to cool for about 1 minute. When the cookies are cool enough to pick up, roll each cookie in the saucer of powdered sugar. Put the cookies back on the plate to cool. When the cookies are completely cool, roll each one in powdered sugar again.

YIELD: 24 snowballs

CHOCOLATE DOLLARS

Wouldn't you love to be a banker in a country where these delicious dollars were used as money?

YOU WILL NEED

A large mixing bowl
A wooden spoon
Ungreased cookie sheets
A flat-bottomed glass
Waxed paper

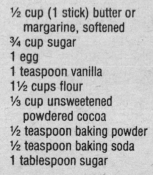

½ cup (1 stick) butter or
     margarine, softened
¾ cup sugar
1 egg
1 teaspoon vanilla
1½ cups flour
⅓ cup unsweetened
     powdered cocoa
½ teaspoon baking powder
½ teaspoon baking soda
1 tablespoon sugar

Put the butter or margarine and the sugar in the mixing bowl, and blend them together using the wooden spoon. Add the egg and vanilla, and stir. Stir in the flour, cocoa, baking powder, and baking soda. Mix thoroughly.

Wrap the dough in plastic wrap or waxed paper and put in the refrigerator to chill for 1 hour. While the dough is chilling, wash the dishes. Put the one tablespoon of sugar onto a small piece of waxed paper and set it aside.

PREHEAT OVEN TO 325 DEGREES

When the dough has chilled, take it out of the refrigerator. With your hands shape it into 1-inch balls. Place the balls on the cookie sheet, leaving 2 inches between each ball.

Dip the bottom of the flat-bottomed glass into the sugar that you have put on the waxed paper. Then press the bottom of the glass onto the cookie balls to flatten them. (The sugar on the glass keeps it from sticking to the cookie dough.) Dip the glass bottom into the sugar after you press each cookie. Put the cookies in the oven and bake for 8 minutes. When the cookies are done, remove the cookie sheet from the oven. Use a pancake turner to lift the cookies from the cookie sheet, and put them on a plate to cool.

YIELD: 30 chocolate dollars

GRANDMA'S PEANUT BUTTER CRISSCROSS COOKIES

The crisscross pattern on top of these cookies looks lke a little tic-tac-toe board. Why not play a game of tic-tac-toe while the cookies bake? There will be a prize at the end for winners and losers alike.

YOU WILL NEED

A large mixing bowl
A wooden spoon
Greased cookie sheets
A fork

¼ cup shortening
¼ cup (½ stick) butter or
   margarine, softened
½ cup peanut butter
½ cup sugar
⅓ cup brown sugar, packed
1 egg
1¼ cups flour
½ teaspoon baking powder
1 teaspoon baking soda

Put the shortening, the butter or margarine, the peanut butter, the sugar, and the brown sugar into the mixing bowl, and blend them together using the wooden spoon. Add the egg and stir. Stir in the flour, baking powder, and baking soda. Mix thoroughly.

Wrap the dough in plastic wrap or waxed paper, and place in the refrigerator to chill for about ½ hour. While the dough is chilling, wash the dishes.

PREHEAT OVEN TO 375 DEGREES

When the dough has chilled, use your hands to form it into 2-inch balls. Place the balls 3 inches

37

apart on the cookie sheet. Using the back of the fork, press a crisscross design into the top of each cookie (see drawing). If the fork sticks on the dough, dip the back of the fork into a little flour before pressing the fork onto the dough.

Put the cookies in the oven and bake for 12 minutes or until they just begin to brown around the edges. Take the cookie sheet from the oven. These cookies are especially delicious when eaten warm.

YIELD: 36 cookies

EASY NO-BAKE TREATS

BUTTERSCOTCH CRUNCHIES

The rich and creamy butterscotch coating on these crunchy cookies makes ordinary breakfast cereal into a mouth-watering treat. Watch them disappear!

YOU WILL NEED

A large saucepan
A wooden spoon
Waxed paper

2 cups (12-ounce package) butterscotch chips
½ cup peanut butter
6 cups corn flakes or other unsweetened cereal flakes

Put the butterscotch chips and the peanut butter into the saucepan. Place over low heat and stir constantly with the wooden spoon until the chips are melted. Remove the pan from the heat and stir in the cereal flakes, making sure the cereal is well coated. Drop the mixture by teaspoonfuls onto a sheet of waxed paper. Let stand 20 minutes.

YIELD: 36 cookies

PEANUT BUTTER CREAMS

These peanutty no-bake treats taste more like a candy than a cookie. You don't need the stove at all to make them.

YOU WILL NEED

A mixing bowl
A wooden spoon
Waxed paper

1 cup peanut butter
1 cup light corn syrup
1¼ cups dry powdered milk
1 cup powdered sugar
1 cup chopped salted peanuts

Put the peanut butter and corn syrup into the mixing bowl. Stir in the powdered milk and the powdered sugar. Use the wooden spoon to mix everything together. Then turn the mixture out of the bowl onto a sheet of waxed paper. Use your hands to knead the ingredients together until they are blended thoroughly. Use your hands to shape the mixture into 1-inch balls. Roll each ball in the chopped peanuts.

YIELD: 48 peanut butter creams

CHOCOLATE CLUSTERS

Once you have tasted these chocolatey mounds your mouth may start to water every time you think of them.

YOU WILL NEED

A large saucepan
A wooden spoon
Aluminum foil

1 cup (6-ounce package) semi-sweet chocolate chips
¾ cup sweetened condensed milk
2 cups dry unsweetened cereal

Put the chocolate chips in the saucepan and place over low heat, stirring constantly with the wooden spoon until the chips are about half melted. Remove from the heat and stir until the chips are melted and smooth. Stir in the sweetened condensed milk. Stir in the dry cereal, making sure that the chocolate mixture evenly coats the cereal pieces. Drop the mixture by teaspoonfuls onto a sheet of aluminum foil and let the clusters harden.

YIELD: 30 clusters

TRUFFALOES

Easy to make and not too sweet, these no-bake bonbons are always a nice addition to a tray of cookies at holiday time.

YOU WILL NEED

A large mixing bowl
A wooden spoon
Waxed paper

2 cups graham cracker crumbs
2 tablespoons unsweetened powdered cocoa
1 cup powdered sugar
1 cup chopped walnuts
2 tablespoons honey
3 tablespoons milk
¼ cup powdered sugar to roll the cookies in

Put the graham cracker crumbs, the cocoa, the cup of powdered sugar, and the chopped nuts in the bowl, and mix together using the wooden spoon. Stir in the honey and milk. The mixture will be dry and crumbly. Use your hands to blend all of the ingredients together to make a dough. When everything is well blended, use your hands to form the dough into 1-inch balls. Put the remaining ¼ cup powdered sugar on the waxed paper and roll the cookie balls in the sugar.

YIELD: 24 pieces

CRISPY CHIP BARS

These crispy bars are so light and airy that you may be shocked by all of the super flavor that they hold. You will want to make these easy treats often.

YOU WILL NEED

A 13 × 9-inch baking pan, greased
A large saucepan
A wooden spoon

1 cup (6-ounce package) semi-sweet chocolate chips
¼ cup (½ stick) butter or margarine
4 cups miniature marshmallows (or 36 large marshmallows)
6 cups puffed rice cereal

Sprinkle the chocolate chips evenly over the bottom of the baking pan. Put the butter or margarine into the saucepan and set over low heat, stirring constantly with the wooden spoon until the butter or margarine melts. Add the marshmallows and continue to heat, stirring constantly, until the marshmallows melt. Remove the pan from the heat. Stir in the cereal, making sure that the cereal is well coated with the melted marshmallow-and-butter mixture. Spread the mixture evenly into the greased pan on top of the chocolate chips. Pack the mixture firmly into the pan using the back of the wooden spoon. Let the mixture cool before cutting into squares.

YIELD: 36 squares

CHOCOLATE GRANOLA DROPS

It may be hard for you to believe that drops this scrumptious are so easy to make. These treats are just what you need for a burst of quick energy.

YOU WILL NEED

A large saucepan
A wooden spoon
Waxed paper

2 cups sugar
½ cup milk
½ cup (1 stick) butter or margarine
3 tablespoons unsweetened powdered cocoa
1 teaspoon salt
3 cups quick, uncooked rolled oats
1 teaspoon vanilla
1 cup shredded coconut
1 cup salted peanuts

Put the sugar, milk, butter or margarine, cocoa, and salt into the saucepan. Place the saucepan over medium heat and stir with the wooden spoon until the mixture comes to a boil. When the mixture begins to boil, take it off the burner, and turn the burner off. Stir in the oats, vanilla, coconut, and peanuts. Drop the mixture by teaspoonfuls onto sheets of waxed paper. Let the cookies stand for about 1 hour to harden.

YIELD: 48 drops

COOKIES FOR
SPECIAL
OCCASIONS

NEW YEAR'S CONFETTI COOKIES

These colorful confetti-topped cookies are a delicious and easy way to welcome the New Year. This is one time that you will prefer to have confetti in your mouth instead of in the air!

YOU WILL NEED

A large mixing bowl
A wooden spoon
Greased cookie sheets
A sheet of waxed paper
A flat-bottomed glass

½ cup shortening
½ teaspoon salt
1 cup sugar
1 egg
2 tablespoons milk
2 cups flour
1 teaspoon baking powder
½ teaspoon baking soda
Multicolored candy sprinkles

PREHEAT OVEN TO 400 DEGREES

Put the shortening, salt, sugar, and egg into the mixing bowl, and use the wooden spoon to blend thoroughly. Stir in the milk, flour, baking powder, and baking soda. Mix well. Put some of the candy sprinkles onto the waxed paper.

Use your hands to shape the cookie dough into 2-inch balls. Dip the top of each ball into the sprinkles. Place the balls sprinkle side up on a greased cookie sheet, leaving 3 inches between each ball. Use the bottom of the glass to flatten out each cookie ball. If the glass sticks to the dough, dip the bottom of the glass into a little sugar before pressing it on the dough.

Put the cookie sheet in the oven and bake the

cookies for about 10 minutes or until the edges of the cookies begin to turn golden brown. When the cookies are done, take the cookie sheet from the oven. Use a pancake turner to lift the cookies off the cookie sheet and onto a rack to cool.

YIELD: 36 cookies

FROSTED B-MY-VALENTINE COOKIES

An edible way for you to say
"Be my friend," on this special day

YOU WILL NEED

A large mixing bowl
A wooden spoon
Ungreased cookie sheets
A rolling pin
Pastry cloth or waxed paper
A heart-shaped cookie cutter,
   or clean cardboard
   and scissors and a small
   pointed knife
A pancake turner

¾ cup shortening
1 cup sugar
2 eggs
1 teaspoon vanilla
2½ cups flour
1 teaspoon baking powder
½ teaspoon salt
Decorator's frosting (see
   below)
Tiny cinnamon candies

Put the shortening, sugar, and eggs in the bowl, and use the wooden spoon to blend them thoroughly. Stir in the vanilla, flour, baking powder, and salt. Wrap the dough in plastic wrap or waxed paper and put it in the refrigerator to chill for at least 1 hour.

49

While the dough is chilling, wash the dishes and clear a space on the counter. If you do not have a heart-shaped cookie cutter, make a model by tracing the sample heart pattern on page 82 onto the clean cardboard. Use the scissors to cut the heart out of the cardboard. When the dough has chilled, take it out of the refrigerator.

PREHEAT OVEN TO 400 DEGREES

Roll out the dough and cut it into heart-shaped pieces. (See "How To Roll and Cut Out Dough for Cutout Cookies" on page 76.) Place the heart-shaped pieces on the cookie sheet. Leave 1 inch between the cookies. Put the cookie sheet in the oven and bake the cookie hearts for about 6 minutes or until the edges of the hearts begin to turn golden brown. When the cookies are done, remove the cookie sheet from the oven and use a pancake turner to put the cookies on a plate to cool.

Use a table knife to spread each cookie with a thin layer of decorator's frosting (see below). Put a cinnamon candy in the center of each heart while the frosting is still wet. Let the frosting dry.

YIELD: 40 cookies

Decorator's Frosting

YOU WILL NEED

A small bowl
A wooden spoon
A table knife

2 cups powdered sugar
¼ cup milk
Red food coloring

Put the powdered sugar into the bowl. Gradually stir in the milk to make a smooth mixture about the consistency of liquid shampoo. Stir in 2 or 3 drops of red food coloring to make the mixture pink.

LINCOLN LOGS

It is claimed that Abraham Lincoln, our 16th president, was born in a log cabin. If the Lincoln cabin had been made of these logs, little Abe probably would have eaten his parents out of house and home.

YOU WILL NEED

A large saucepan
A wooden spoon
A 13 × 9-inch baking pan,
   greased

4 ounces (4 squares)
   unsweetened chocolate
1 cup (2 sticks) butter or
   margarine
4 eggs
2 cups sugar
1 teaspoon vanilla
1¼ cups flour
1 teaspoon baking powder
Fudge frosting (see below)

PREHEAT OVEN TO 350 DEGREES (325 IF YOU USE A GLASS PAN)

Put the chocolate and butter or margarine into the saucepan. Place over low heat and stir with the wooden spoon until the butter or margarine has melted. Remove the pan from the heat and stir until the chocolate has melted. Stir in the eggs, sugar, vanilla, flour, and baking powder. Mix thoroughly.

51

Spread the batter evenly into the greased pan. Place the pan in the oven and bake for 35 minutes or until the batter begins to pull away from the sides of the pan. Remove the pan from the oven and let the cookies cool in the pan for about 45 minutes.

When the cookies are cool, spread them with the fudge frosting while they are still in the pan. Smooth out the frosting. Then take a fork and drag the tines along the length of the frosting to make it look like tree bark. Let the frosting set before cutting the cookies into bars.

YIELD: 36 logs

Fudge Frosting

YOU WILL NEED

A small mixing bowl
A wooden spoon
A table knife
A fork

⅓ cup butter or margarine, softened
⅓ cup unsweetened powdered cocoa
2 cups powdered sugar
1 teaspoon vanilla
2 tablespoons milk

Put the butter or margarine into the bowl and use the wooden spoon to blend in the cocoa. Gradually stir in the powdered sugar and vanilla. Stir in the milk after you have added about half of the sugar. Then add the rest of the sugar, and stir all of the ingredients together until smooth. If the frosting is too thick add a little more milk to thin it out.

52

WASHINGTON'S CHERRY DROPS

The story goes that George Washington cut down a cherry tree when he was a lad. Maybe he was just trying to get fruit for these chocolate cherry drops.

YOU WILL NEED

A large mixing bowl
A wooden spoon
Greased cookie sheets

½ cup (1 stick) butter or
    margarine, softened
½ cup sugar
1 egg
½ teaspoon vanilla
1 cup flour
¼ cup unsweetened
    powdered cocoa
½ cup maraschino cherries,
    cut up

PREHEAT OVEN TO 350 DEGREES

Put the softened butter or margarine into the bowl. Blend in the sugar using the wooden spoon. Stir in the egg and vanilla. Then stir in the flour and the cocoa. Mix thoroughly. Stir in the cut-up cherries. Drop the dough by teaspoonfuls one inch apart onto the greased baking sheet. Bake the cookies for 12 minutes or until they start to become firm. When the cookies are done, use a pancake turner to lift them from the cookie sheet onto a rack to cool.

YIELD: 36 cookies

ST. PATRICK'S DAY SHAMROCKS

Legend says that St. Patrick drove the snakes out of Ireland. If the snakes had known about these green cookies, they might have been more reluctant to leave.

YOU WILL NEED

A large mixing bowl
A wooden spoon
Ungreased cookie sheets
Clean scissors

½ cup (1 stick) butter or
   margarine, softened
¼ cup sugar
Green food coloring
1½ cups flour
Black licorice sticks

PREHEAT OVEN TO 350 DEGREES

Put the softened butter or margarine into the mixing bowl. Use the spoon to blend the sugar into the butter or margarine. Stir in 4 to 5 drops of green food coloring. Blend in the flour and mix well. The dough should look and feel like "play doh."

With your hands take ½ teaspoon of the dough and mold it into a ball. Repeat, making all of the dough into little balls. Use the scissors to cut the licorice into 1-inch pieces. These will be the shamrock "stems."

Take three of the dough balls and put them together in a triangle on the cookie sheet. Use your fingers to flatten the balls and press the dough together. Put the licorice stem at the bottom and press the dough down on the licorice.

Repeat with the rest of the dough balls until you have used up all of them. If you have one or two balls left over, add them to one of your 3-leaf shamrocks to make a lucky 4-leaf clover.

Put the cookies in the oven and bake for 8 minutes or until the edges of the cookies begin to turn golden brown.

When the cookies are done, take the cookie sheets from the oven. Allow the cookies to cool before removing them from the cookie sheets.

YIELD: 24 shamrocks

55

EASTER BUNNY NESTS

These little white nests filled with jelly bean "eggs" will make a colorful centerpiece for the table that you can eat when dinner is over.

YOU WILL NEED

A mixing bowl
An electric mixer or an egg beater
A wooden spoon
A heavy brown-paper bag
Clean scissors

2 egg whites (see page 89 for how to separate egg whites)
¼ teaspoon cream of tartar
½ cup sugar
1 cup shredded coconut
36 jelly beans

PREHEAT OVEN TO 275 DEGREES

Put the egg whites into the mixing bowl and allow them to warm up to room temperature. Use the electric mixer or the egg beater to beat the egg whites until they are foamy. Beat in the cream of tartar. Gradually beat in the sugar, a little at a time. Continue beating until the mixture is stiff. The mixture is ready when it will form stiff peaks when dropped from a spoon. Use the wooden spoon to stir in the coconut.

Cut a piece of brown paper from the bag that will just cover the bottom of the cookie sheet, and put it on the cookie sheet.

Drop the egg-sugar-and-coconut mixture by teaspoons onto the brown paper to form 12 equal piles. Use the back of the spoon to shape each pile to look like a nest. Put the cookie sheet into the oven and bake for 40 minutes. When the 40 minutes are over, turn off the oven but leave the cookies in the oven for 1 more hour. After 1 hour, take the cookies out of the oven and carefully peel the cookie nests off of the brown paper. Put 3 jelly beans in each nest.

YIELD: 12 nests

NOTE These cookies should not be frozen.

MAYPOLES

Use your imagination to make these buttery treats in all kinds of spring colors.

YOU WILL NEED

A large mixing bowl
A wooden spoon
A small bowl
Ungreased cookie sheets
Waxed paper

1 cup shortening
1 cup powdered sugar
1 egg
1 teaspoon almond extract
1 teaspoon vanilla
2½ cups flour
Green and yellow food
 coloring

PREHEAT OVEN TO 375 DEGREES

Put the shortening and sugar into the large mixing bowl and blend together using the wooden spoon. Stir in the egg, almond extract, and vanilla. Stir in the flour. You may have to use your hands to get the flour all mixed in. Divide the dough in half. Leave half of the dough in the big bowl and put the other half in the small bowl.

Add 4 or 5 drops of green food coloring to one bowl of dough. Use your hands to mix the color in evenly. Add 4 or 5 drops of yellow food coloring to the dough in the other bowl, kneading the color in evenly. Pinch off a piece of green dough and roll it between your hands to make a snake about 3 inches long. Put it down on a piece of waxed paper. Pinch off a piece of yellow dough and make another snake the same size. Twist the two snakes together to make a green-and-yellow-striped maypole about 3 inches long. Repeat, using the rest of the dough until all the dough has been made into maypoles.

Put the maypoles about 1 inch apart on the cookie sheet and bake for about 8 minutes. Don't let the cookies get brown.

YIELD: 36 maypoles

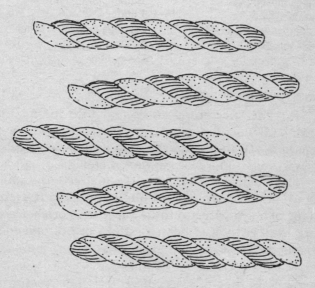

NOTE The maypole dough looks and feels a lot like "play doh." It molds the same way, too. For different cookies, try forming flower petals out of the yellow dough and use the green dough for stems and leaves. You can also use different colors of food coloring to dye the dough to make pink tulips, purple violets, and red roses. Bake as you would for the maypoles.

FIRECRACKERS

Red-licorice fuses help make these fireworks not only legal but also welcome at any Fourth of July celebration.

YOU WILL NEED

A large mixing bowl
A wooden spoon
Ungreased cookie sheets
Clean scissors
Waxed paper

½ cup shortening
¼ cup sugar
1½ cups flour
Red licorice whips
Red-colored decorator's
 sugar

PREHEAT OVEN TO 350 DEGREES

Put the shortening and sugar into the mixing bowl, and use the wooden spoon to blend them together. Stir in the flour to make a soft dough. Put the red sugar on a piece of waxed paper.

Cut the licorice whips into 4-inch lengths. Take about a tablespoon of the dough and mold it in the shape of a cylinder around a piece of licorice. Make sure that ½ inch of licorice sticks out of one end. This is the "fuse."

Roll each cylinder in red sugar and place each one on the cookie sheet. Leave 2 inches between each cookie. Put the cookies in the oven and bake for about 7 minutes or until the edges of the cookies look golden brown. Let the cookies cool on the cookie sheet for 5 minutes before removing them from the sheet.

YIELD: 36 firecrackers

COLUMBUS'S SPICE DROPS

Everyone knows that Christopher Columbus convinced King Ferdinand and Queen Isabella of Spain to give him money for his voyages by promising to bring back spices from the Orient. You can celebrate Columbus's discoveries by baking these cookies made from the spices he was seeking.

YOU WILL NEED

A large mixing bowl
A wooden spoon
Greased cookie sheets

PREHEAT OVEN TO 400 DEGREES

½ cup shortening
½ cup sugar
½ cup light or dark molasses
1 egg
⅓ cup water
2 cups flour
2 teaspoons baking soda
1 teaspoon ground ginger
1 teaspoon ground cinnamon
1 teaspoon ground cloves

Put the shortening, sugar, molasses, egg, and water into the mixing bowl. Stir with the wooden

61

spoon to blend them together. Stir in the flour, baking soda, ginger, cinnamon, and cloves. Mix well. Drop by tablespoonfuls onto a greased cookie sheet. Leave 2 inches between each cookie. Put in the oven and bake for about 8 minutes or until the cookies start to become firm.

Take the cookie sheet from the oven and allow the cookies to cool before removing them from the cookie sheet.

YIELD: 36 spice drops

WITCHES' HATS

Devil's-food brims and milk-chocolate peaks join to form these Halloween treats.

YOU WILL NEED

A large mixing bowl
A wooden spoon
Greased cookie sheets

½ cup shortening
1 cup sugar
1 egg
1¼ teaspoons baking soda
1 teaspoon vanilla
½ cup unsweetened
   powdered cocoa
2 cups flour
1 cup milk
36 chocolate kisses,
   unwrapped

PREHEAT OVEN TO 375 DEGREES

Put the shortening, sugar, and egg into the bowl, and blend together using the wooden spoon. Stir in the baking soda, vanilla, and cocoa. Stir in the flour and milk. Mix well. Drop the dough by teaspoonfuls onto a greased cookie sheet. Leave 2 inches between each cookie. Press a chocolate kiss onto the top of each cookie.

Put the cookie sheet into the oven and bake for 12 minutes or until the edges of the cookie bottoms begin to brown. Use a pancake turner to tip a cookie to see underneath. When the cookies are done take the cookie sheet from the oven. Let the cookies cool before removing them from the cookie sheet.

YIELD: 36 cookies

GINGERBREAD PEOPLE

Gingerbread people are a traditional holiday cookie that everyone loves. By using different decorations and frostings on your gingerbread people, you can make them look young or old, happy or sad, funny or scary. You can even decorate them to look like people you know.

YOU WILL NEED

A large mixing bowl
A wooden spoon
A rolling pin
A pastry cloth or waxed paper
A cookie cutter, *or* clean
    cardboard and scissors
    and a small pointed knife
A table knife
A pancake turner
Ungreased cookie sheets

½ cup shortening
½ cup sugar
½ cup light or dark molasses
¼ cup water
2½ cups flour
½ teaspoon salt
½ teaspoon baking soda
1 teaspoon ground ginger
1 teaspoon ground cinnamon
½ teaspoon ground cloves
Cinnamon candies
Raisins
Gum drops
Decorator's frosting (see
    page 50)

Put the shortening, sugar, molasses, and water into the mixing bowl, and blend together using the wooden spoon. Stir in the flour, salt, baking soda, ginger, cinnamon, and cloves. Mix well. Wrap the dough in plastic wrap or waxed paper and put the dough into the refrigerator for 1 hour to chill.

If you do not have a cookie cutter shaped like a person, trace the sample pattern on page 81 and use the scissors to cut it out. With the pattern make a cardboard model. When the dough has chilled 1 hour, take it out of the refrigerator.

PREHEAT OVEN TO 375 DEGREES

Roll and cut the dough to make gingerbread people, and place them on the cookie sheet (see "How To Roll and Cut Out Dough for Cutout Cookies," page 76). Leave 2 inches between each cookie. Put the cookie sheets into the oven and bake for 10 minutes or until the edges of the cookies just begin to brown. Remove the cookies from the oven and allow them to cool for 15 minutes before decorating. You can leave the cookies right on the cookie sheets while you decorate them.

To decorate Use the decorator's frosting to make clothes on the people. Spread the frosting very thin, using a table knife. Use raisins and cinnamon drops for eyes, buttons, or mouths. The most important thing to use is your imagination. Make each gingerbread person special, with a personality all his or her own.

YIELD: 16 gingerbread people

FUN
WITH
COOKIES

Now that you have mastered the basic techniques of cookie baking in this book, a whole new kind of fun begins!

FANCY CUTOUT COOKIES

To make Valentine cookies, use the recipe for Frosted B-My-Valentine Cookies on page 49.

To make gingerbread people, use the recipe for Gingerbread People on page 64.

To find the recipe for Decorator's Frosting, see page 50.

If you do not have cookie cutters, use the sample patterns beginning on page 80.

The recipe for B-My-Valentines makes a basic sugar-cookie dough that can be cut into any shape you want, and decorated in as many ways as you can think of. Here are some ideas for fancy cutout cookies. You can think of lots more!

Easter Eggs Cut the dough into egg shapes and bake as directed in the recipe. When the cookies have cooled, use several different colors of decorator's frosting to make gaily painted Easter eggs.

Shamrocks Cut the dough into the shape of a clover. Bake as directed in the recipe. When the cookies have cooled, frost them with decorator's frosting that has been colored green.

Jack-o'-Lanterns Cut the dough into the shape of a pumpkin with a stem. Bake as directed in the recipe. When the cookies have cooled, ice them with decorator's frosting that has been colored orange. Use mini-size chocolate chips for the eyes, nose, and mouth.

Christmas Trees Cut the dough into the shape of a tree, and bake as directed in the recipe. When the cookies have cooled, frost them with decorator's frosting that has been colored green. Use small candies for ornaments, and a little coconut for snow.

The dough used for Gingerbread People also can be cut into different shapes. Instead of people, make dogs or cats, trees, or even a house. Use decorator's frosting to paint on ears and eyes, windows, and chimneys.

A decorating tip It is easy to make thin lines with decorator's frosting if you use a small brush. Buy a brush that comes to a good point, like the kind you would use to paint watercolors. Use it ONLY for painting frosting onto cookies. With a brush you can be a cookie artist, and you can eat your works of art when you are done!

PERSONALIZED COOKIES

Your family, friends, and guests will feel extra special if you write their names on cookies with frosting "ink." Personalized cookies also make great place cards for dinner or a party.

Use flat, smooth cookies, like Double Fudge Brownies (page 14), Blonde Brownies (page 15), Peanut Butter Bars (page 16), or Frosted B-My-Valentines (page 49).

First write the name on paper, so you will know how big or small to make the letters on the cookie.

Put some white decorator's frosting (page 50) into a small plastic sandwich bag. Squeeze the frosting down into one corner of the bag. Use clean scissors to snip a very tiny piece off the filled corner of the bag. Then squeeze the frosting through the tiny opening in order to write. Practice writing on waxed paper a few times before you write on the cookie.

DRESSED-UP COOKIES

You may want your cookies to look extra-super-special sometimes. With a little imagination you can really dress them up. Here are a few ways to do it. You can think of more.

Columbus's Spice Drops (See page 61.) When the cookies have cooled, dip the top of each cookie into white decorator's frosting (page 50). Place a piece of cherry or a tiny candy on top of the icing and allow it to dry.

Lincoln Logs (See page 51.) After you have frosted the logs and cut them into bars, put two little pieces of green gumdrop and a piece of red candy on top of each bar to turn the Lincoln Logs into Yule Logs.

Peanut Butter Bars (See page 16.) Frost the cookies with fudge frosting (page 52) before cutting them into bars. Then cut them into bars and place a peanut or two on top of each one.

Snowballs (See page 34.) When the Snowballs have cooled, dip the top of each one into decorator's frosting (page 50) that has been colored blue or yellow. Put a tiny candy on top of each one.

Chocolate Dollars (See page 35.) Brush a little water on each cookie when they are cool. Then place a paper doily on each cookie. Sprinkle with powdered sugar. When you lift off the doily, there will be a pretty sugar pattern on the cookie.

COOKIE-AND-ICE-CREAM SANDWICH SNACKS

Most cookie lovers are also ice cream lovers. When you put cookies and ice cream together, you have a match made in heaven!

Use cookies that are thin and flat, like Molasses Chews (page 31), Chocolate Dollars (page 35), New Year's Confetti Cookies (page 48), Giant Chocolate Chippers (page 22), Grandma's Peanut Butter Crisscross Cookies (page 37), or Gingerbread People (page 64).

On a piece of waxed paper, set out two cookies for each sandwich that you want to make. Turn the cookies upside down, so the flat side is face up.

For each sandwich, put a scoop of ice cream on the flat side of one cookie, and place the flat side of another cookie on top. Press down. Wrap each sandwich in waxed paper or plastic wrap and immediately put the sandwiches in the freezer. They should be in the freezer for at least a half hour before you serve them.

Here are some suggestions for kinds of sandwiches. Maybe you'll invent some of your own.

Grasshoppers Use Chocolate Dollars, with mint-chocolate-chip ice cream for the filling.

Mr. Chips Use Giant Chocolate Chippers, with chocolate-chip ice cream for the filling.

Peanut Butter Sandwich Use Grandma's Peanut Butter Crisscross Cookies, with strawberry ice cream for the filling.

Chew Chews Use Molasses Chews, with vanilla ice cream for the filling.

The Fat Man Use Gingerbread People, with vanilla ice cream for the filling.

Confruiti Use New Year's Confetti Cookies, with strawberry ice cream for the filling.

ELEGANT COOKIE DESSERTS

Cookies can be fabulous when you use them in desserts. Chewy bar cookies are best for these dessert treats because they are almost like super-moist cake.

Brownies a la Mode Follow the recipe for Double Fudge Brownies (page 14). Cut into 12 large bars. For each serving, pour 2 tablespoons of canned chocolate syrup on a plate. Put a brownie in the syrup. Place a scoop of vanilla ice cream on top of the brownie. Then pour 2 more tablespoons of chocolate syrup over the ice cream.

Toffee Teasers Follow the recipe for Tropical Toffee Bars (page 17). Cut into 12 large bars. For each serving, place a bar on a plate. Put a scoop of vanilla ice cream on top of the bar. Pour 2 tablespoons of butterscotch sauce (you can use prepared sauce, from a jar) over the ice cream.

Brownies with raspberries Follow the recipe for Double Fudge Brownies (page 14). Cut into 12 large bars. Let a package of frozen raspberries thaw by putting them on a low shelf in the refrigerator for a few hours. For each serving, put 2 tablespoons of the raspberry juice on a plate. Place a brownie in the raspberry juice. Put a scoop of vanilla ice cream on top of the brownie. Then spoon some of the thawed raspberries over the ice cream.

A COOKIE PARTY

Since you love to bake and eat cookies, you probably know other cookie lovers. Why not plan a cookie party with a few friends? Here is one way to do it.

Decide how many people to invite. Invite them well in advance, because they are going to need time to bake cookies!

Ask each guest to bake his or her favorite kind of cookie, and to bring to the party 2 cookies for each person who will be there, including you. It's more fun if everyone brings a different kind of cookie.

Arrange to have small, empty bags or boxes, one for each of your guests. You can decorate the bags or boxes.

As the guests arrive, ask them to put one of their cookies into each bag or box, and the rest on a plate. This way everyone will get to try each kind of cookie while they are at the party and will have another one of each kind to take home.

If you really want to go cookie crazy, bake a big batch of cutout cookies before your guests arrive. Make small bowls of different colored decorator's frosting (page 50). Give each guest a table knife and plenty of space to work, and have a cookie-frosting jamboree!

For a cookie party the refreshments are simple. Since the guests have supplied the cookies, you only have to supply something good to drink, plus plenty of napkins and hospitality.

HOW TO ROLL AND CUT OUT DOUGH FOR CUTOUT COOKIES

To roll the dough use a rolling pin or a straight-sided jar.

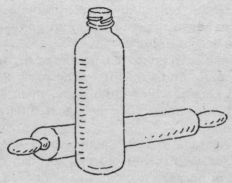

To cut out the dough, use a cookie cutter or a cardboard pattern and a small pointed knife.

Prepare a surface to roll on. Use any one of the following: a pastry cloth; a pastry board made of metal, wood, or marble; or a piece of waxed paper spread on a flat table or countertop.

Sprinkle flour liberally over the rolling surface. This will prevent dough from sticking after cookies are cut.

Place a large piece of dough in center of rolling surface. Flatten dough slightly with your hand.

Rub flour on rolling pin or jar. Start in center of dough and roll out toward the edge of the dough. Continue rolling evenly until dough is about ¼-inch thick.

Dust cutter or cardboard pattern with flour. Cut as close to edge of dough as possible. With cutter, press down firmly. With pattern, use the pointed knife to cut around the shape. Do not lift up the cut dough yet. Continue to cut out cookies until entire rolled sheet of dough has been cut.

With your fingers, peel away the dough around the cut cookies. Set the scraps aside to be rerolled and cut later.

Use the pancake turner to gently lift the cut-out cookie dough off of the rolling surface and onto the cookie sheet.

Gather all the scraps of dough and press them firmly together to make a ball. Sprinkle flour on rolling surface. Roll and cut dough as before. Continue until all the dough has been used.

SAMPLE PATTERNS FOR CUTOUT COOKIES

These patterns can be used in place of cookie cutters. First trace the pattern onto a piece of paper and cut it out. Lay the paper pattern on a piece of clean cardboard and cut around it to make a cardboard pattern. Use the cardboard pattern for making the cookies. (See the illustration on page 76.)

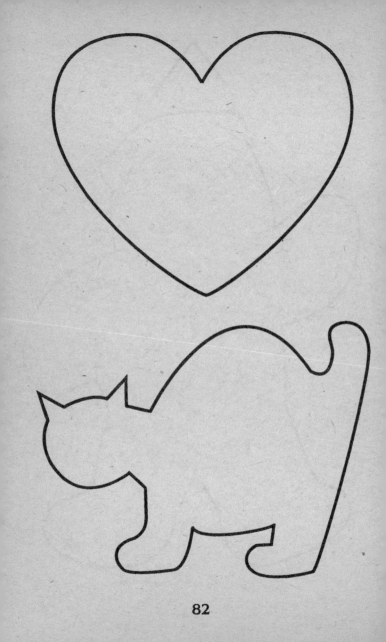

INGREDIENTS AND UTENSILS

(INCLUDING SOME HELPFUL HINTS)

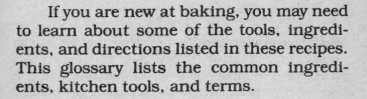

If you are new at baking, you may need to learn about some of the tools, ingredients, and directions listed in these recipes. This glossary lists the common ingredients, kitchen tools, and terms.

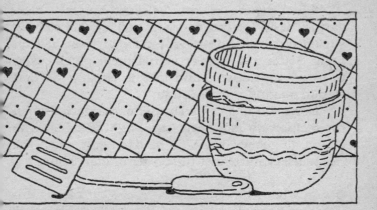

INGREDIENTS

Baking powder Baking powder is a white powder used to help baked goods fill with air as they bake. It usually comes in a can. Do not confuse it with baking soda, which is explained below.

Baking soda Baking soda is a white powder used to help cookies and other baked goods rise, or fill with air, while they bake. Baking soda usually comes in a box. Do not confuse baking soda with baking powder, which is explained above. They act differently in recipes, and if you use the wrong one the recipe may not work.

Butter or margarine Most of these recipes specify "butter or margarine." They taste about the same when used to bake cookies. No matter which one you choose, make sure it is the plain, lightly salted kind; don't use the kind that is whipped.

When the recipe says "softened butter or margarine," it means butter or margarine that has been sitting out of the refrigerator for at least half an hour. Softened butter or margarine is much easier to blend with sugar, and that is usually the first step in making cookie dough.

Don't ever use melted butter or margarine when the recipe says "softened." Melting it will make the dough all gooey; it should be done only when the recipe tells you to melt the butter or margarine.

Cocoa When the recipe says "cocoa," it means unsweetened powdered cocoa. It usually comes in a can. Do not confuse this with sweetened cocoa mix that is used to make chocolate milk or hot chocolate. Pure cocoa has no sweetener in it; if you taste a little bit on your finger, it will be very bitter.

Coconut For these recipes, "coconut" means shredded, sweetened coconut. It comes in a bag or a can. (If you have fresh, shredded coconut it will work fine, too, but it will not be quite as sweet.)

Egg whites Some of the recipes in this book specify the use of egg whites. To separate the egg white from the egg yolk for those recipes, do the following:

Take out two small bowls. Crack the egg shell on the side of one of the bowls. The egg shell should break in half. Carefully pass the egg yolk back and forth from one half of the broken shell into the other half of the shell, allowing the egg white to drip down into the bowl.

When all of the egg white has fallen away from the egg yolk, put the egg yolk into the second bowl. Then put the egg white that you have gathered into the mixing bowl for your recipe.

Never drip egg white into a bowl that already is holding the white of another egg. If the yolk of the second egg breaks while you are separating the white, both egg whites will be ruined.

The leftover yolks can be saved for a day or two in the refrigerator to use in an omelet.

Flour The recipes in this book use plain white flour, also known as all-purpose flour. Do not use whole wheat flour, self-rising flour, or cake flour in these recipes. The recipes will not work with them.

Graham cracker crumbs These are just that what they sound like—crumbs made from graham crackers. You can't always buy graham cracker crumbs, so it's usually easier to make your own. Take graham crackers and put them between two sheets of waxed paper. Then use a rolling pin or the back of a wooden spoon to smash them into little crumbs.

Shortening If a recipe says "shortening," it means vegetable shortening. Vegetable shortening comes in a can. It is solid but soft, and is usually white or light yellow.

Sugar Three different kinds of sugar are used in these recipes. Always used the kind specified for the recipe.

If the recipe just says "sugar," it means regular white sugar, also known as granulated sugar.

If the recipe says "brown sugar," it refers to a heavy dark sugar that has a different flavor from regular sugar. Brown sugar can be light brown or dark brown. Either kind will work fine in these recipes. To measure brown sugar, pack it firmly into the measuring cup so there are no air holes in the sugar.

If the recipe says "powdered sugar," it means a fine, white, powdery sugar, also called confectioner's sugar. This is the sugar usually used for frosting. If you are using powdered sugar in a recipe, make sure that there are no lumps in it. If the sugar is lumpy, put it through a sieve before you use it.

Unsweetened chocolate This kind of chocolate is used for baking. It usually comes in little 1-ounce squares, individually wrapped in paper. Like cocoa, it has no sugar in it and is very bitter.

Vanilla When a recipe says "vanilla," it means vanilla extract. Vanilla extract comes in a little bottle. It is made from vanilla beans. If you have vanilla beans in your house, leave them alone. You do not need them for these recipes.

UTENSILS

The recipes in this book list certain utensils that you will need to make the dough and bake the cookies. Here are the basics.

Baking pans Baking pans can be made of glass or of metal (usually aluminum). If you use a glass pan, lower the oven temperature for baking by 25 degrees. Three different sizes of baking pans are used in these recipes:

13 × 9 × 2—an oblong pan with low sides

9-inch-square pan—9 inches on each side and 2 inches deep

8-inch-square pan—as deep as the 9-inch-square pan, but only 8 inches long on each side

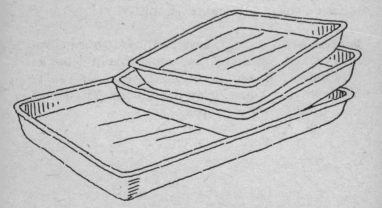

Cookie sheets Flat metal sheets used to bake cookies. Cookie sheets have either very low sides or no sides at all. This makes it easier to take the cookies off the sheet when they are done. For some recipes, the cookie sheet is used just as it is. But if a recipe says to use a greased cookie sheet, rub a small amount of shortening all over the top surface of the sheet with a bit of waxed paper before you put the cookie dough onto the sheet.

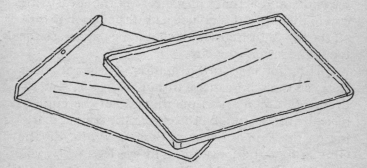

Greased pans Some of these recipes say to use a "greased pan." To grease a pan, put a little shortening on a piece of waxed paper. Then rub the paper all over the inside of the pan (the bottom and sides) until the inside is covered with a thin film of shortening. Cookies sheets are also greased this way.

Measuring cups Measuring cups are special cups used to measure amounts that are more than 4 tablespoons. There are two kinds of measuring cups:

Cups for measuring dry ingredients, like flour, sugar, nuts, and crumbs. They are usually made of plastic or aluminum. These will say right on the cup how much they hold. For these recipes you will need a ¼-cup measure, a ⅓-cup measure, a ½-cup measure, and a 1-cup measure. Fill the measuring cup to the top and then use a knife or spoon to even off the top. Your ingredient should be flat across the top of the measuring cup.

Cups for measuring liquids. These cups are clear, so that you can see through them. The measurements are marked on the side of the cup. To measure any liquid, fill the cup to the correct marking on the side of the cup. Bend down (or lift the cup) so that the marking is at eye level when you read the measure.

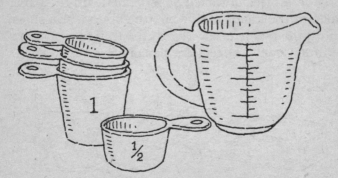

Measuring spoons There are special spoons for measuring. They usually come on a ring, and each is marked to indicate exactly how much it holds. For these recipes you will need a ¼-teaspoon measure, a ½-teaspoon measure, a 1-teaspoon measure, and a 1-tablespoon measure. All the recipes in this book refer to level measurements. Make sure that the ingredient being measured fills the spoon and is flat across the top.

Mixing bowl A big bowl with high sides for mixing the dough. A 10-inch (diameter) bowl is a good size for these recipes, because it allows plenty of room for stirring in the flour.

Rack A wire or metal rack is useful to place hot cookies on when they are removed from the oven. You lift the cookies from the hot cookie sheet with a pancake turner and put them on the rack. The rack allows air to circulate around the cookies, helping the cookies cool.

Saucepan Just a pan with a handle, like the kind you use for cooking vegetables. A 2-quart size is best for the recipes in this book because it is big enough to hold all the batter and still give you room to stir.

Wooden spoon Almost all of the recipes in this book tell you to use a wooden spoon to mix the dough. The reason is that wooden spoons are the easiest spoons to work with. They have a large surface. They don't bend under pressure, and a good wooden spoon will not break from cookie making. If you don't have a wooden spoon you can use some other kind of big spoon, but it won't be as easy.

NOTE All of the cooking times and temperatures in this book are designed to be performed in a conventional oven. Do not try these recipes in a microwave oven. They simply won't work.
